Polar Bears
For Kids

Amazing Animal Books for Young Readers

By Kim Chase

Mendon Cottage Books

JD-Biz Publishing

Download Free Books!
http://MendonCottageBooks.com

Read More Amazing Animal Books

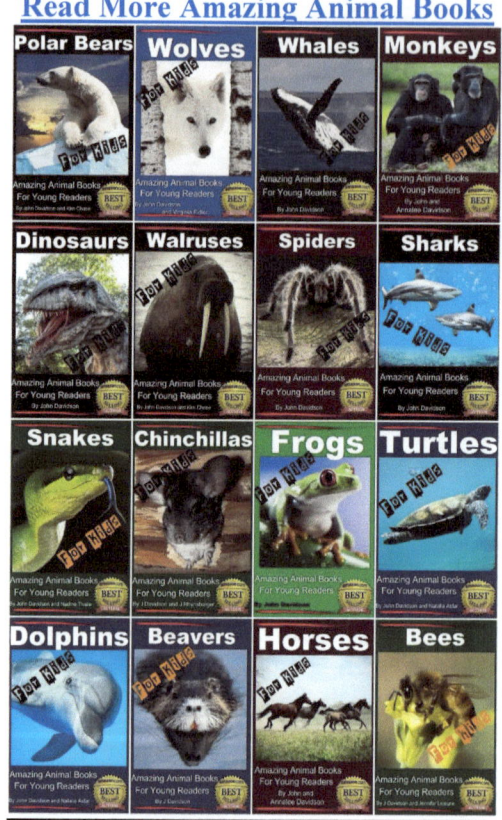

Purchase at Amazon.com

Download Free Books!
http://MendonCottageBooks.com

Table of Contents

Introduction 4

About Polar Bears 5

Polar Bears 7

What Polar Bears Do 10

How Polar Bears Communicate 13

Baby Polar Bears 15

Polar Bear Facts 17

Where to Polar Bears Live 19

Arctic Polar Bears 21

Why are the Polar Bears Endangered 23

What Polar Bears Eat 25

Habitat of Polar Bears 28

Other Names for Polar Bears 30

Photo Credits 34

Read More Amazing Animal Books 35

Publisher 41

Introduction

Have you ever wondered about the world of the polar bears? Wondered about things like where do they live, or what do they eat? Did you know that polar bears communicate with each other? You may have seen pictures of polar bears many times, but what do you really know about them? Are polar bears really white?

There are so many interesting things to learn about these powerful bears!

About Polar Bears

When polar bears live outdoors in the wild, they can live to be about 15 to 18 years old. However, there have been some bears recorded to have been as old as 31 or 32 years old. Polar Bears that live in captivity (not living in the wild) can many times live to be between 35 – 39 years old. In fact, there was a female polar bear that lived to the age of 42 in a Canadian zoo!

Polar bears are very smart. In fact, a research scientist claimed that polar bears are every bit as smart as apes. A hungry polar bear was observed smashing open blocks of ice to get to the fish that were frozen inside. These bear can be playful as well. Some bears were observed stacked up plastic pipes, just to knock them all down again.

To help the polar bear survive in the Arctic, they need to rely on their senses. They have very good hearing and eyesight, as well as a good sense of smell. Their teeth are very sharp and spaced far apart. This helps them when they eat, and to hold onto their prey.

Polar Bears

Surprisingly, even though a polar bear may appear white, they really aren't! Polar bears have a dense fur that locks in their body heat. This fur is an undercoat that is topped with guard hairs. Each hair shaft has a core that is hollow, and actually reflects and scatters the light. The hair shafts are also transparent and color free.

Polar bears appear at their most white when they are in sunlight, and clean. This is especially true after their molt period. This molt period starts in the spring, and ends by the late part of summer. Before the molting begins, the oils the bears eat from the seals make them appear yellow in color.

Polar bears actually have black skin! Under this skin, is a layer of blubber that measures about 4 ½ inches thick. It is the bear's fur, and not their blubber that stops the bears from losing any of their body heat. Adult male polar bears can overheat quickly when they run.

A polar bear's paw can measure about 12" across. These paws help the polar bears to spread their weight evenly when they are trying to get across thin ice. If the polar bears find themselves on a patch of really thin ice, they can distribute their weight even more. This is done when they move their bodies closer to the ice, and reach their legs farther apart. When it comes time for them to stalk their prey, they are masters at knowing exactly where to place each paw, as they move quietly along. When polar bears are swimming, they use their front paws for paddling, and their hind paws help to steer them. Of all the bears, the only one that can be considered to be a marine mammal is the polar bear.

Under each paw, the polar bears have black footpads. There are soft, small bumps on these footpads called papillae. The papillae help the polar bears hold onto the slippery ice as they try to walk across. Polar bears usually move slowly, and would rather walk on snow than on ice. The male polar bears have been measured at usually walking between speeds of 3 – 4 mph. Mother polar bears when walking with her cubs, walk even slower than that. They will walk between 1 ½ to almost 2 mph. For a very short distance, polar bears can run as fast as horses, being clocked at nearly 25 miles per hour!

The claws of the polar bear are curved, strong, thick and sharp. Each claw is over two inches in length. The claws of the polar bears are used for many things. Their claws help them to grip the ice as they make their way across. These claws also help them to grab and hold onto their prey.

Polar bears have compact, short tails, and rounded small ears. These features help the bears to keep in their body heat.

What Polar Bears Do

Polar bears like to keep themselves dry and clean. One reason for this is that if their fur becomes matted down, dirty and wet, it will be hard for them to keep in their body heat.

During the summer, the bears will eat for about 20 – 30 minutes, and then they head out for open water. Once in the water, they can spend nearly 15 minutes cleaning themselves by washing themselves off. Another thing they also do to keep clean is to lick their muzzles, chests and paws.

Since wet fur does not insulate them against the cold, how do polar bears dry themselves off? They begin by shaking the extra water off, and then they rub their wet fur in the snow.

During the wintertime, the polar bears will use the snow to clean themselves off instead of using the water. It is almost funny to watch the bears as they try to clean themselves.

They start by rubbing their massive head in the snow then they push along forward on their bellies, and finish up by rolling on their backs.

A mother polar bear will lick her cubs to keep them clean. Her cubs will help to keep themselves clean by licking themselves as well as the other cubs. Once the cubs leave their den, they begin learning how to wash themselves both in the water and in the snow.

Sleeping is another important thing that polar bears do. These bears can sleep between seven and eight hours in one day, plus they like to take naps also.

Polar bears spend their spring and summertime on the ice. There on the ice, you can find the polar bears sleeping much more during the daylight hours than during the nighttime. It is believed the reason for this is that the seals tend to be more active at night. But in this area of the Arctic where there is 24 hours of sunlight during the summer, followed by 24 hours of darkness during the winter, it would be hard for the polar bears to be able to tell the difference between day and night.

Polar bears have the ability to nap nearly at any time, and anywhere. This is especially true after they eat. Bears save up their energy by napping.

How Polar Bears Communicate

Polar bears can actually speak to each other. They use both vocal sounds and body language. When a polar bear moves their head from side to side, this is called head wagging, and it is a sign that they want to play. When an adult bear wants to play, they will stand up on two feet, and lower their chin down into their chest, and have their front paws down at their side.

On the other hand, when a polar bear is angry, they let out loud growls or roars. A deep growling sound may be used as a warning to help protect their food. An aggressive polar is one that has their head lowered and can be heard making snorting or hissing sounds. When a polar bear attacks, they have their ears pinned back, with their heads down, as they charge forward. A polar bear that does not want to fight, will avoid the more dominate bears by staying downwind of them, so that the more aggressive bears do not catch their scent.

A Mother polar bear can make a few different sounds when "talking" with her cubs. If a Mother bear is not happy with a cub, she can scold the cub with a low growling sound. If she is worried about the safety of her cubs, she can give out a short chuffing sound. Should a male polar bear come too close to her or her cubs, she will lower her head and rush towards him. This is her way of giving off a warning, and letting the male bear know to go away and not to come any closer.

Baby Polar Bears

Before a baby polar bear is born, the mother makes them a place to live. This home is called a den. She starts making the den in the fall. These dens are made in a number of places. Some dens are made in snowdrifts in hills close to shore. Other dens are made in snowdrifts found alongside mountain slopes. Still other dens are dug in snowdrifts found on sea ice.

The mother will spend the whole winter in the den. Once springtime comes, the mother will leave the den, and her new little cubs will follow her. The bears usually leave their den in March or April. The mother polar bear will spend the next 2 ½ years with her cubs. It has been noted that some polar bears moms in the Hudson Bay area do separate themselves from their young only after 1 ½ years. During this time, she will teach her cubs how to hunt, and she will protect them from harm.

A mother polar bear usually gives birth to twins during the winter months of November or December. But there have also been reports of a single cub being born, or as many as three (triplets) cubs born to a litter.

Newborn polar bear cubs weigh only about one pound when they are born. They measure about 12" to 14" in length. These little cubs rely totally on their mother both for food and for warmth. Newborns are born blind, and without any teeth, but they are born with soft, short fur.

From the time that they are born, until they are a year old, these polar bear babies are known as coys. After being a coy, the polar bear moves on to being known as a cub. It is not until these cubs leave their mothers and are ready to start their own family, that they are called subadults.

Polar Bear Facts

Polar bears are built to stand up to the freezing cold Arctic temperatures. They actually have not one, but two fur layers as well as a thick layer of fat to help them to keep warm. The polar bear's fur and skin soak up the sunlight and help protect them from the cold water. When polar bears swim, they use their big front paws to push them through the water, and they steer with their back legs. Polar bears are also excellent swimmers, and have been recorded to swim 100 miles at a time. It may seem odd, but polar bears run more of a risk of overheating after they run, than they do of trying to keep warm!

Polar bears also have a strong sense of smell. This is important for when they are hunting and trying to find seals. Their claws are very powerful. Polar bears can grab seals that weigh between 150 to 200 lbs. right out of the water!

The only predator the polar bears have are humans. On land, the polar bear is the biggest predator, and the polar bears are the biggest of all the bears. Ursus maritimus is the scientific name given to the polar bears. The meaning is "sea bear."

The adult male polar bear can weigh anywhere between 720 to 1,200 lbs., and can grow to a height of ten feet when standing on its hind legs! Think of it. That is the size of a building that is one story high! The largest recorded polar bear was a male that weighed in at 2,209 lbs! An adult female can weigh anywhere between 500 to 600 lbs.

When scientists refer to the height of polar bear, they are measured this way: The polar bear is measured from the shoulders, and when they are down on all fours, not standing on their hind legs. So remembering how they are measured, the average height of an adult polar bear is estimated between 3 ½ to 5 feet for either female or male.

Where to Polar Bears Live

Polar Bears live to the far north in the Arctic where it is very cold. They can be found living in five nations. These nations are: Alaska (which is part of the United States), Greenland, Canada, Norway and Russia.

Polar bears live on sea ice, and along the shores of the frigid Arctic. Sea ice is formed over the ocean in the colder weather. Many of the polar bears go out on this sea ice to hunt for food, usually seals. There have been reports of polar bears being spotted hundreds of miles away from the nearest shore! Once the warmer weather returns, the sea ice begins to melt. When the sea ice starts melting, the polar bears head back to the shore.

It is believed by Scientists that polar bears live in their own very distinct areas known as home ranges. The home range of a polar bear can be huge, and bigger than any of the other bear species. There was one Alaskan bear's range that was measured to be 45 times larger than the area of the Great Smoky Mountains National Park. A park of that size is home to about 400 black bears.

A polar bear's home range size will depend largely on the amount of food that is available in that area. In an area where there is a good supply of food, the polar bear's home range will be smaller, and many times overlap the home range of other bears.

Once a subadult polar bear leaves their mother, they could travel over 600 miles in order to set up their new home range. Scientists do believe that many of these bears will limit their home range travel to a few hundred miles. But there are always exceptions to every rule as this female bear can prove. One amazing female bear was tracked by satellite and set off on an incredible journey covering 3,000 miles! She started out from Prudhoe Bay in Alaska. Then is was on to Greenland, followed by Ellesmere Island in Canada, and then back to Greenland once again.

Arctic Polar Bears

One interesting fact about polar bears is that they only live in the areas of the Arctic surrounding the North Pole. Polar bears do not live in Antarctica, an area surrounding the South Pole. Often times in illustrations, polar bears and penguins are seen together. But in real life, this wouldn't happen. Penguins live in the Antarctic.

Arctic is a word that comes from a Greek word meaning bear. The Arctic is where polar bears live. The word **Antarctic** on the other hand, comes from a Greek word meaning without bear. These two places are in the direct opposite of each other!

October is the month when the sun sets in the High Arctic. The sun will not rise again until later in the month of February. Here, the temperatures will plummet to below –50F and will stay near that frigid temperature for days or even weeks. –29F is the average temperature during the months of January and February. But even in these unbelievably cold temperatures, the polar bear's body temperature will remain at 98.6F thanks to their excellent insulation.

Why are the Polar Bears Endangered

Many animals that live in the coldest areas on earth share in one common problem, and the polar bear is no exception to this rule. That problem is the rise in temperature. These warmer temperatures are believed to be as a result of global warming. The result of this warming trend is the decrease in the amount of sea ice. This is the polar bears biggest threat.

Sea ice plays a very important role in the life of a polar bear. They need this ice when they hunt their prey, such as seals, and some bears choose to make their den on the ice. The polar bears just couldn't survive without sea ice. Even though the polar bears are good, strong swimmers, when the sea ice melts it can create a very big problem. The polar bears are forced to swim further and for a longer period of time. These longer swims can prove too much for the younger cubs, and sadly, some do not make that long journey in search of their much needed sea ice. The cubs do not have enough body fat, and because of this, it is hard for them to stay afloat in the water, and they become more exposed to the cold.

In the Arctic during the summer melt off, a great deal of sea ice is lost then. To give you an idea of just how much ice is lost, it would be equal to the size of the states of Washington, Alaska, and Texas all together!

As if that wasn't enough, the polar bears must deal with other things as well. These bears also have the added problems of poaching, pollution, and the effect that industries have on where they live.

If the current threats to their environment do not change, it is felt that the world will lose two-thirds of its polar bear population by the middle of the century, and all of the remaining polar bears by the century's end.

What Polar Bears Eat

Seals are the polar bears main source of food. When seals swim underwater for a long time, they need to come to the surface to breathe. They make holes in the ice for this very reason. These holes are known as breathing holes. Many times, the polar bears will wait quietly at these breathing holes, just waiting for the seal to surface. Then, once the seal surfaces, the polar bear will pounce on its prey.

Other times, the polar bears may stalk the prey. When they spot a seal resting on the ice, the bears will move slowly towards the seal. If a seal should raise their head to look at the polar bear, the bear will stand perfectly still. Then when the polar bear gets close enough, at about 20 feet, they charge or pounce at the seal.

Another way the polar bear captures its prey is by hunting it while swimming below the icy surface. Although this may sound cruel, the polar bears do play an important role in nature. They keep the balance in nature by not having too many seals. The polar bears keep the seal population in balance so that there will be enough food to go around.

When the polar bears eat, what they are feeding on is the seal fat, or blubber from the seals. This seal fat is the highest possible calorie source of food for them. The two types of seals they hunt for are the bearded and the ringed seals. The ringed seals are smaller, and easier to catch for the female and younger polar bears. The bearded seals are larger, and hunted by many of the male bears.

During times when there is plenty of food to be found, the polar bears will eat just the seal fat. In fact, they can eat as much as 100 lbs. of blubber at one time! This fat or blubber helps the polar bear to build up the reserve of fat they need to live off of for in between meals. The seal's carcass is left for scavengers in this region, like younger polar bears, ravens, or Arctic foxes.

Polar bears rely on the ice for their main food source, seals. In the summer months when the ice floes move back, there are some bears that will follow these ice floes. Sometimes, they will travel hundreds of miles just to stay close to their food supply. Polar bears that become trapped on land in the summer months must stay on land until the fall when the ice will form again. For those bears trapped on land, they will face a summer with little food to eat. It is rare that they will be able to catch any seals in the open water.

Polar bears may eat other foods, but that is only once in a while. Usually these other foods do not have the calories needed to keep the bears alive. Exceptions to this would be a beached whale or a walrus. Because of the polar bear's huge body size, they need a great number of calories to stay alive, and to build up their own fat.

A polar bear may actually share the carcasses that they find. There is usually one bear in charge of the carcass. They will share their meal with another bear, if the other polar bear asks properly. This is done when the bear wishing to eat approaches the polar bear in charge by walking on all fours close to the ground. They then slowly walk, circling the carcass, and finish by touching their nose to the nose of the leader bear.

Habitat of Polar Bears

Polar bears actually love the freezing cold temperatures of the Arctic! Temperatures in the wintertime can plummet to –50F. But the polar bears are ready for this. During the winter, they will sleep in the shallow pits that they dug out of the snow.

Polar bears can sleep through a blizzard from their beds they made on a ridge. If a polar bear makes their sleeping spot on the leeward side of the ridge, they will be protected them from the winds. As they sleep, piles of snow mount on top of the bears. But this snow actually acts like a blanket that will insulate them, and help to keep them warm. Polar bears may decide sometimes to wait out the storm, and just stay there, curled up beneath the snow. It may take a few days before the storm finally passes.

During the summer, polar bears have been known to curl up on a patch of ice, and use their paw or an ice block as their pillow. Polar bears that are further inland, and not near the water, will often dig themselves sleeping pits. These sleeping pits are dug along the shoreline either in the gravel ridges, or in the sand.

Other Names for Polar Bears

The name we know for this interesting, large white bear is polar bear. But did you know that the polar bear has many other names too? As we learned earlier, the scientific name for the polar bear is Ursus maritimus. The meaning is sea bear. An officer named Commander C. J. Phipps, who was part of the British Navy, gave this name to the polar bear back in the year 1774. He wrote a book titled, "A Voyage toward the North Pole", and it was in this book that the name Ursus maritimus was first used and seen.

After that, there was a Greek scientific name that was widely used for the polar bear. That name was Thalarctos. The meaning came from two different Greek words. The word thalasso, means sea and the word arctos, means bear of the north. The scientific name Thalarctos stayed for quite a while. But in 1971, it was decided to return to the original name given to the polar bear, and Ursus maritimus was used once again.

The people that live near the polar bears have a deep respect for them, and they each have their own special name that they call them.

Nanuk is the name given to the polar bears by the Eskimos and Inuit. When they write poetry about the polar bears, they refer to them as ever wandering one, or Pihoqahiak.

Beliy medved is the Russian name, and it means white bear.

Isbjorn is the name given to the polar bear by the people of Denmark and Norway. The meaning is ice bear.

In Norse poetry, the polar bears have been described as the rider of icebergs, white sea deer, the sailor of the floe, the whale's bane, and the seal's dread. The poets were quick to praise the polar bears and compared them to men. They would write that the polar bears were as smart as 11 men, and had the strength of 12.

The farmer was the name given to them by the whalers of the nineteenth century. The polar bears got that name because of their turned in feet (known as pigeon toed) and their slow walk.

A Siberian tribe known as the Ket calls the polar bear "Gyp", which means grandfather. They also call them "Qoi", which is the word for stepfather.

The Sami people will never say the real name for the polar bear. The reason for this is that they would never want to offend him. So instead, they have other names they use when they refer to polar bears. These names are old man in the fur cloak, or God's dog.

Tornassuk is the name given to the polar bear by the people of eastern Greenland. The meaning is master of helping spirits.

As you can see, there are many names given to these wonderful, powerful, white looking bears that roam the Arctic region!

Photo Credits

Polar bear in natural environment

© *Vladimir Melnik - Fotolia.com*

Polar she-bear with cubs.

© *Uryadnikov Sergey - Fotolia.com*

Polar bear in natural environment

© *Vladimir Melnik - Fotolia.com*

eisbär

© *Marcus Mantel - Fotolia.com*

Polar bear

© *erectus - Fotolia.com*

Polar bear

© *erectus - Fotolia.com*

Cub of polar bear under mother protection

© *andamanec - Fotolia.com*

Fighting polar bears.

© *Uryadnikov Sergey - Fotolia.com*

Polar Bear Catches Fish

© *GVision - Fotolia.com*

Polar bear in natural environment

© *Vladimir Melnik - Fotolia.com*

Read More Amazing Animal Books

Purchase at Amazon.com

Horses For Kids
Amazing Animal Books For Young Readers
By John and Annalee Davidson

Ponies For Kids
Mendon Cottage Books
Amazing Animal Books
For Young Readers
Rachel Smith

Ten Amazing Horses For Kids
Nature Books for Kids
JD-Biz Publishing
K. Bennett

Akhal-Teke "The Golden Horse of the desert" For Kids
Nature Books for Kids
JD-Biz Publishing
K. Bennett

Suffolk-Punch "The Gentle Giant" For Kids
Nature Books for Kids
JD-Biz Publishing
K. Bennett

Shires "The great Horse" For Kids
Nature Books for Kids
JD-Biz Publishing
K. Bennett

Colonial Spanish "Horse of the Americas" For Kids
Nature Books for Kids
JD-Biz Publishing
K. Bennett

Canadian "The Little Iron Horse" For Kids
Nature Books for Kids
JD-Biz Publishing
K. Bennett

Cleveland Bays "History and Future" Horses For Kids
Nature Books for Kids
JD-Biz Publishing
K. Bennett

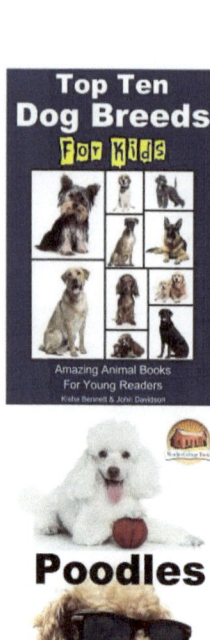

Top Ten Dog Breeds For Kids

Amazing Animal Books For Young Readers

Kisha Bennett & John Davidson

German Shepherds

Dog Books for Kids
K. Bennett

Bulldogs

Dog Books for Kids
K. Bennett

Dachshund

Dog Books for Kids
K. Bennett

Poodles

Dog Books for Kids
K. Bennett

Labrador Retrievers

Dog Books for Kids
K. Bennett

Rottweilers

Dog Books for Kids
K. Bennett

Boxers

Dog Books for Kids
K. Bennett

Golden Retrievers

Dog Books for Kids
K. Bennett

Puppies

Dog Books For Kids

Amazing Animal Books
By John Davidson

Beagles

Dog Books for Kids
K. Bennett

Yorkshire Terriers

Dog Books for Kids
K. Bennett

Dogs
Top Ten Dog Breeds For Kids

Amazing Animal Books For Young Readers

Zahra Jazeel & John Davidson

Cats For Kids

Amazing Animal Books For Young Readers
K. Bennett & John Davidson

Foxes For Kids

Amazing Animal Books For Young Readers
Zahra Jazeel & John Davidson

Wolves For Kids

Amazing Animal Books For Young Readers
By John Davidson and Virginia Fidler

Monkeys — Amazing Animal Books For Young Readers — By John and Annalee Davidson

Whales — Amazing Animal Books For Young Readers — By John Davidson

Kittens — Amazing Animal Books For Young Readers — By John Davidson

Meerkats For Kids — Amazing Animal Books For Young Readers — John Davidson and Lisa Barry

Elephants For Kids — Amazing Animal Books For Young Readers — Kim Chase & John Davidson

Big Mammals of Yellowstone For Kids — Amazing Animal Books For Young Readers — By John Davidson

Big Cats For Kids — Amazing Animal Books For Young Readers — By John Davidson

My First Book About Pandas — Amazing Animal Books — By Annalee and John Davidson — BEST — Children's Picture Books

Chinchillas — Amazing Animal Books For Young Readers — John Davidson and Jamie Rhynsburger

Beavers For Kids — Amazing Animal Books For Young Readers — By J Davidson

Bees For Kids — Amazing Animal Books For Young Readers — By J Davidson and Jennifer Lejeune

Animals of Australia For Kids — AUSTRALIA — Amazing Animal Books For Young Readers — By John Davidson and Shawn Vincent Wilson

Frogs For Kids — Amazing Animal Books For Young Readers — By John Davidson

My First Book About Frogs — Amazing Animal Books For Young Readers — By John Davidson — Children's Picture Books

Tigers For Kids — Amazing Animal Books For Young Readers — Kim Chase & John Davidson

Scorpions For Kids — Amazing Animal Books For Young Readers — John Davidson

Snakes For Kids — Amazing Animal Books For Young Readers — By John Davidson and Nadine Thiele

Animals of Africa For Kids — Amazing Animal Books For Young Readers — Steve Muluri & John Davidson

Dinosaurs For Kids — Amazing Animal Books For Young Readers — By John Davidson

Sharks For Kids — Amazing Animal Books For Young Readers — By John Davidson

Spiders For Kids — Amazing Animal Books For Young Readers — By John Davidson

Giant Panda Bears — Amazing Animal Books For Young Readers — By John Davidson

Giraffes For Kids — Amazing Animal Books For Young Readers — Valeria Arcas & John Davidson

Eagles For Kids — Amazing Animal Books For Young Readers — Nicholas Williams & John Davidson

Bears For Kids — Amazing Animal Books For Young Readers — Zahra Jazval & John Davidson

Our books are available at

1. Amazon.com
2. Barnes and Noble
3. Itunes
4. Kobo
5. Smashwords
6. Google Play Books

Download Free Books!
http://MendonCottageBooks.com

Publisher

JD-Biz Corp

P O Box 374

Mendon, Utah 84325

http://www.jd-biz.com/

Mendon Cottage Books

P O Box 374, Mendon Utah 84325